ANIMAL
Infographics

Chris Oxlade

raintree

Raintree is an imprint of Capstone Global Library Limited, a company incorporated in England and Wales having its registered office at 7 Pilgrim Street, London, EC4V 6LB – Registered company number: 6695582

www.raintreepublishers.co.uk
myorders@raintreepublishers.co.uk

Text © Capstone Global Library Limited 2014
First published in hardback in 2014
Paperback edition first published in 2015
The moral rights of the proprietor have been asserted.

Edited by Rebecca Rissman, Dan Nunn, and John-Paul Wilkins
Designed by Philippa Jenkins
Original illustrations © Capstone Global Library Ltd 2014
Illustrations by HL Studios
Picture research by Elizabeth Alexander
Production by Vicki Fitzgerald
Originated by Capstone Global Library Ltd
Printed and bound in China

ISBN 978 1 406 27209 3 (hardback)
17 16 15 14 13
10 9 8 7 6 5 4 3 2 1

ISBN 978 1 406 27214 7 (paperback)
18 17 16 15
10 9 8 7 6 5 4 3 2 1

British Library Cataloguing in Publication Data
Oxlade, Chris.
Animals. – (Infographics)
A full catalogue record for this book is available from the British Library.

Acknowledgements
We would like to thank the following for permission to reproduce photographs: Capstone Global Library p. 4; Shutterstock pp. 4 (© M.Stasy, © Pakhnyushcha, © Stella Caraman, © Thomas Bethge).

We would like to thank Diana Bentley and Marla Conn for their invaluable help in the preparation of this book.

Every effort has been made to contact copyright holders of any material reproduced in this book. Any omissions will be rectified in subsequent printings if notice is given to the publisher.

Disclaimer
All the internet addresses (URLs) given in this book were valid at the time of going to press. However, due to the dynamic nature of the internet, some addresses may have changed, or sites may have changed or ceased to exist since publication. While the author and publisher regret any inconvenience this may cause readers, no responsibility for any such changes can be accepted by either the author or the publisher.

CONTENTS

Some words are shown in bold,
like this. You can find out what they
mean by looking in the glossary.

ABOUT INFOGRAPHICS

An infographic is a picture that gives you information. Infographics can be graphs, charts, maps, or other sorts of pictures. The infographics in this book are about animals.

Infographics make information easier to understand. We see infographics all over the place, every day. They appear in books, in newspapers, on the television, on websites, on posters, and in adverts.

Here is a simple infographic about pets. It shows the number of different pets in the United States.

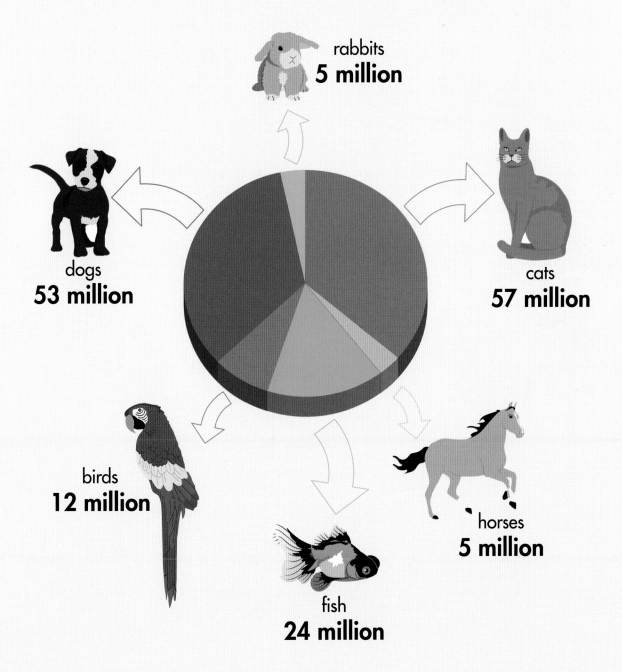

rabbits
5 million

cats
57 million

dogs
53 million

birds
12 million

horses
5 million

fish
24 million

SIZE AND SHAPE

Big animal facts

The blue whale and the African elephant are two of the world's biggest animals. These infographics present some amazing facts about them.

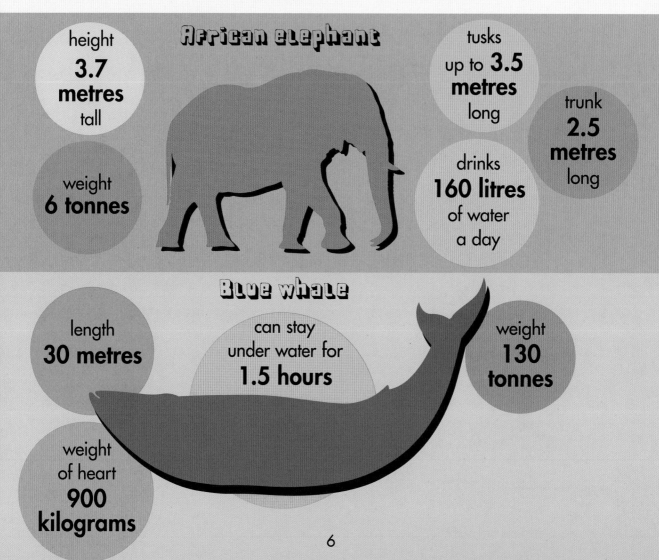

African elephant

height
3.7 metres tall

tusks
up to **3.5 metres** long

trunk
2.5 metres long

weight
6 tonnes

drinks
160 litres of water a day

Blue whale

length
30 metres

can stay under water for **1.5 hours**

weight
130 tonnes

weight of heart
900 kilograms

Comparing weights

How many elephants are equal to a blue whale?
This chart compares the weights of different animals.

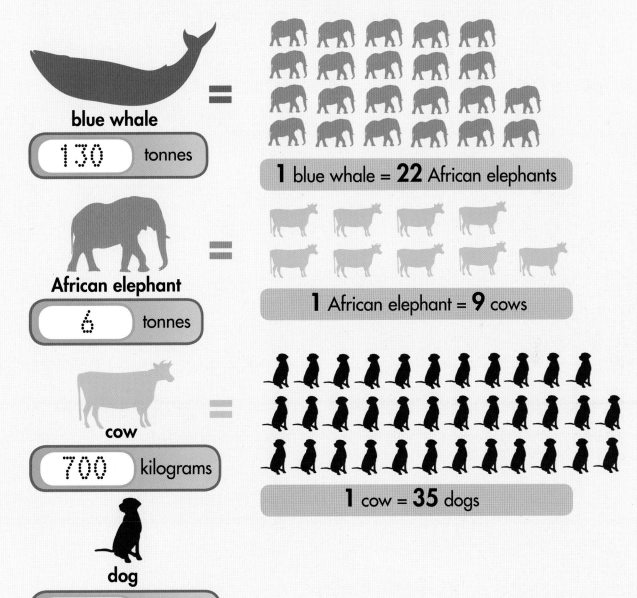

blue whale

| 130 | tonnes |

1 blue whale = **22** African elephants

African elephant

| 6 | tonnes |

1 African elephant = **9** cows

cow

| 700 | kilograms |

1 cow = **35** dogs

dog

| 20 | kilograms |

The biggest animals

We put animals into different groups, such as mammals and birds. This chart shows the biggest animals in different animal groups.

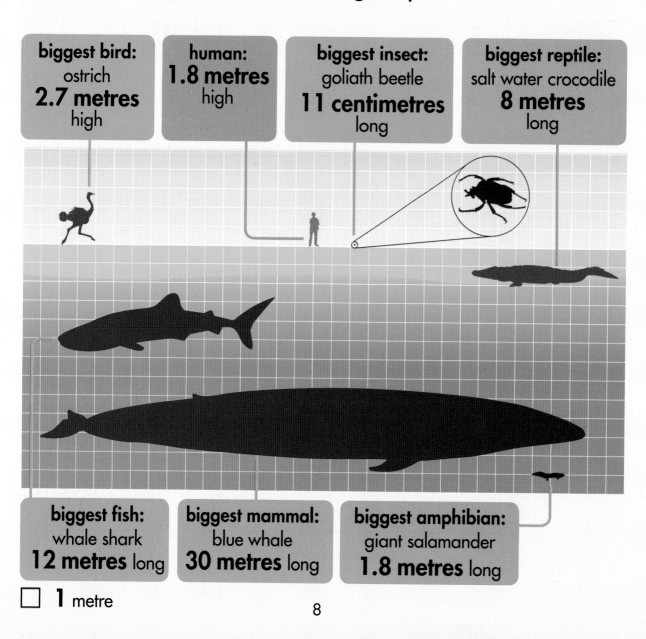

biggest bird:
ostrich
2.7 metres high

human:
1.8 metres high

biggest insect:
goliath beetle
11 centimetres long

biggest reptile:
salt water crocodile
8 metres long

biggest fish:
whale shark
12 metres long

biggest mammal:
blue whale
30 metres long

biggest amphibian:
giant salamander
1.8 metres long

☐ **1** metre

The smallest animals

This chart shows you the smallest animals.
You can see the size of each animal compared to
an adult human's hand.

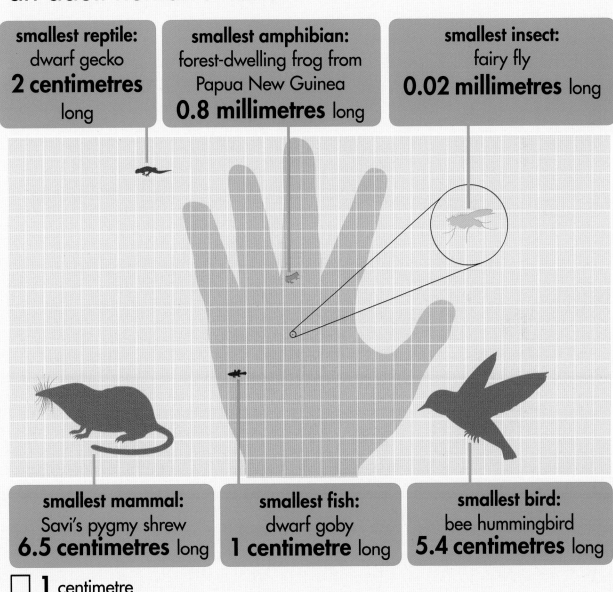

smallest reptile:
dwarf gecko
2 centimetres
long

smallest amphibian:
forest-dwelling frog from
Papua New Guinea
0.8 millimetres long

smallest insect:
fairy fly
0.02 millimetres long

smallest mammal:
Savi's pygmy shrew
6.5 centimetres long

smallest fish:
dwarf goby
1 centimetre long

smallest bird:
bee hummingbird
5.4 centimetres long

☐ **1** centimetre

The longest snakes

This bar chart shows the lengths of the five longest snakes in the world.

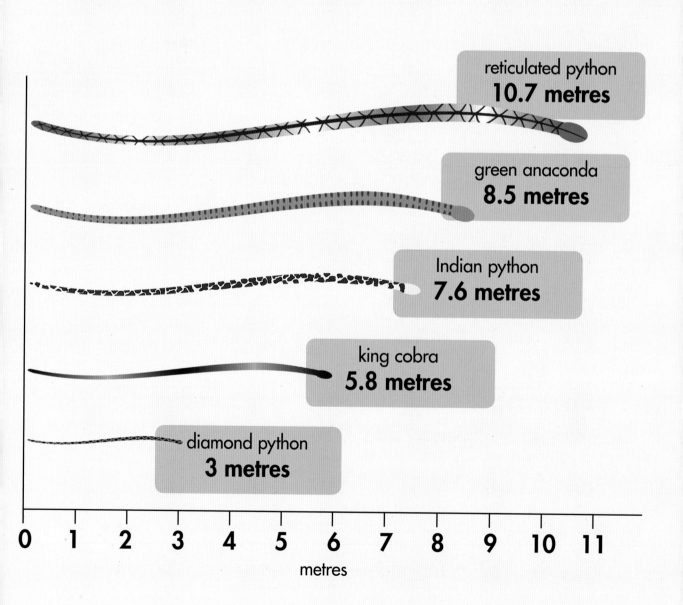

reticulated python
10.7 metres

green anaconda
8.5 metres

Indian python
7.6 metres

king cobra
5.8 metres

diamond python
3 metres

0 1 2 3 4 5 6 7 8 9 10 11

metres

Big insects

The biggest insects are very big! This chart shows the sizes of some of the biggest insects.

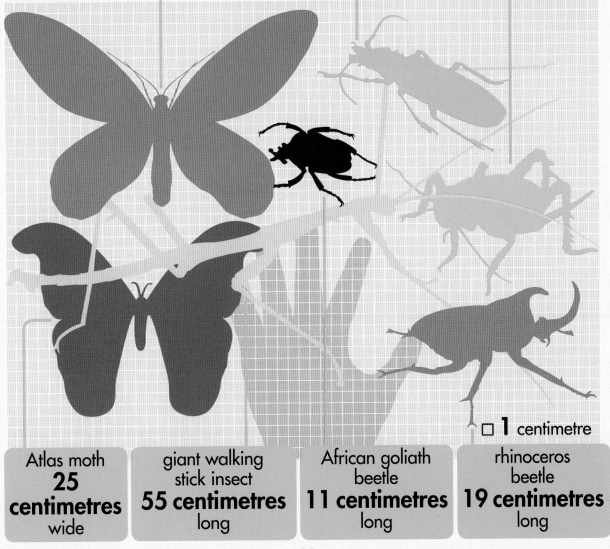

giant birdwing butterfly
29 centimetres wide

Amazonian giant titan beetle
18 centimetres long

giant weta bug
20 centimetres long

Atlas moth
25 centimetres wide

giant walking stick insect
55 centimetres long

African goliath beetle
11 centimetres long

rhinoceros beetle
19 centimetres long

□ **1** centimetre

MOVING ANIMALS

Fastest on land

This chart shows the top speeds of some of the fastest animals on land.

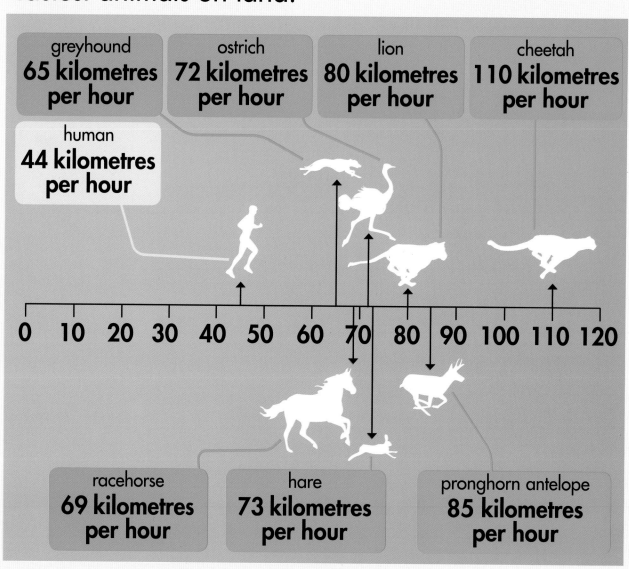

greyhound
65 kilometres per hour

ostrich
72 kilometres per hour

lion
80 kilometres per hour

cheetah
110 kilometres per hour

human
44 kilometres per hour

0 10 20 30 40 50 60 70 80 90 100 110 120

racehorse
69 kilometres per hour

hare
73 kilometres per hour

pronghorn antelope
85 kilometres per hour

The fastest in the air

This chart shows some of the fastest fliers in the air.

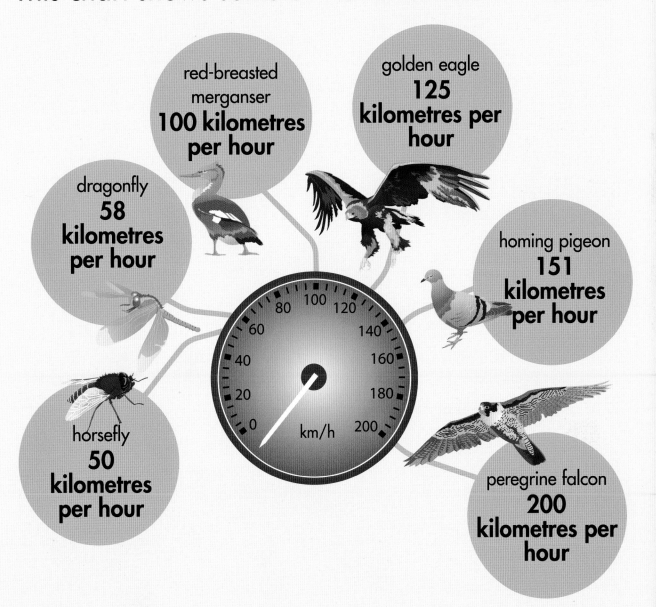

red-breasted merganser
100 kilometres per hour

golden eagle
125 kilometres per hour

dragonfly
58 kilometres per hour

homing pigeon
151 kilometres per hour

horsefly
50 kilometres per hour

peregrine falcon
200 kilometres per hour

Slow animals

Some animals move very slowly. This chart shows how many minutes and seconds some of the slowest animals take to travel 1 metre.

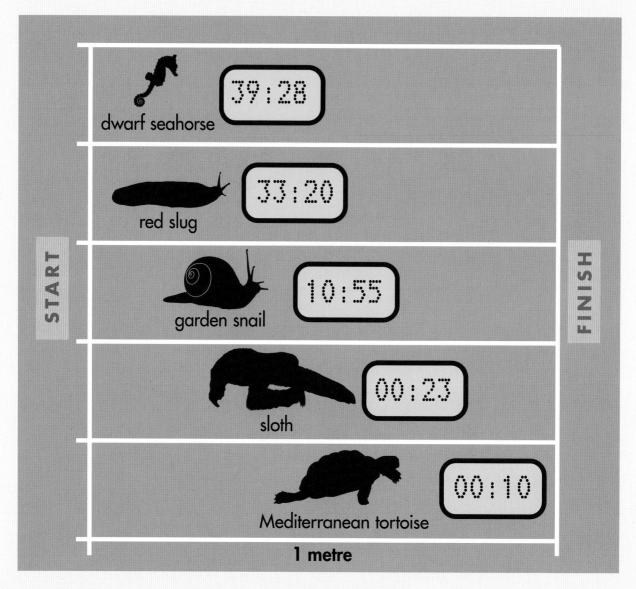

START

dwarf seahorse — 39:28

red slug — 33:20

garden snail — 10:55

sloth — 00:23

Mediterranean tortoise — 00:10

FINISH

1 metre

High jump and long jump

Some animals can jump amazingly high and far. This chart shows some of the best animal jumpers, compared to the best human jumpers.

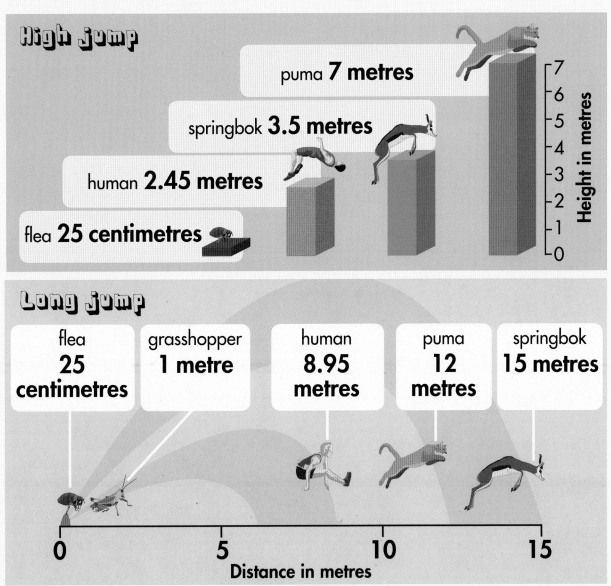

High Jump

puma **7 metres**

springbok **3.5 metres**

human **2.45 metres**

flea **25 centimetres**

Height in metres

7
6
5
4
3
2
1
0

Long Jump

| flea **25 centimetres** | grasshopper **1 metre** | human **8.95 metres** | puma **12 metres** | springbok **15 metres** |

0 — 5 — 10 — 15

Distance in metres

ANIMAL FEATURES

Biggest eyes

Some animals have enormous eyes. This chart shows the widths of the biggest animal eyes, with a human eye to compare them with.

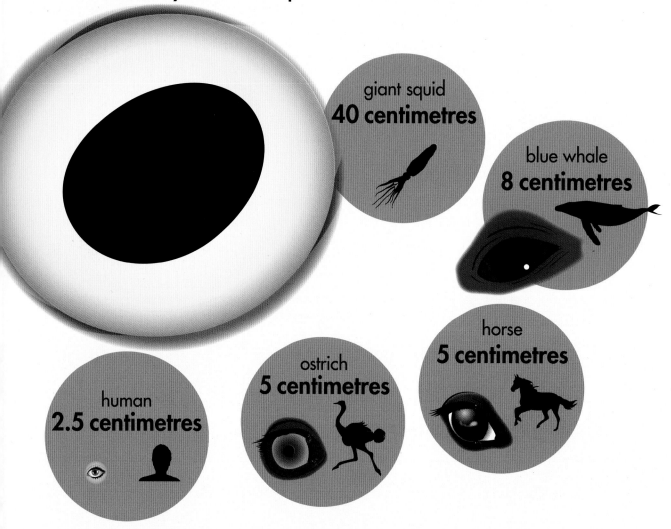

giant squid
40 centimetres

blue whale
8 centimetres

horse
5 centimetres

ostrich
5 centimetres

human
2.5 centimetres

The biggest teeth

This chart shows the lengths of the biggest animal teeth. They make human teeth look tiny!

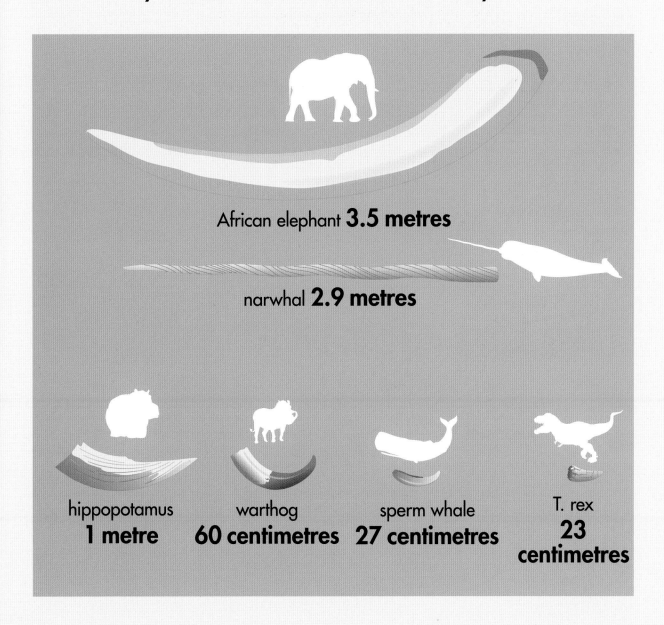

African elephant **3.5 metres**

narwhal **2.9 metres**

hippopotamus **1 metre**

warthog **60 centimetres**

sperm whale **27 centimetres**

T. rex **23 centimetres**

NUMBERS OF ANIMALS

Food chains

Animals have to eat plants and other animals to live. Animal diets can be shown in diagrams called food chains. This food-chain pyramid shows how many other animals or plants need to live in the same place for each animal to survive.

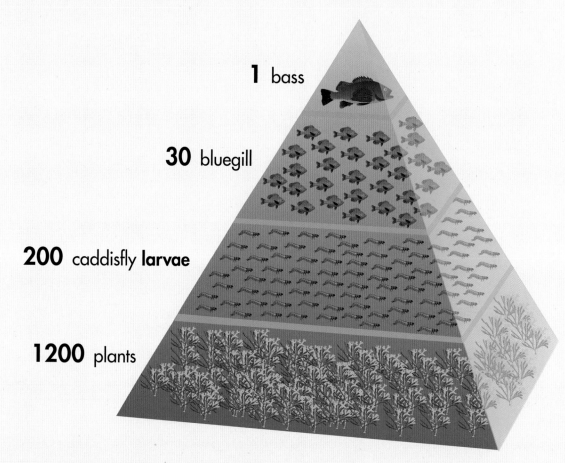

1 bass

30 bluegill

200 caddisfly **larvae**

1200 plants

Animals in danger

Many animals around the world are hunted so much that there are almost none left. Or their habitats are being lost. This chart shows some of these **endangered** animals.

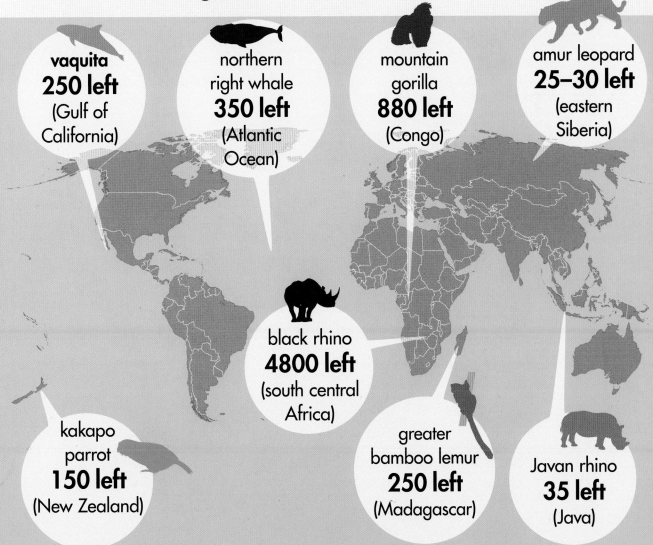

vaquita
250 left
(Gulf of California)

northern right whale
350 left
(Atlantic Ocean)

mountain gorilla
880 left
(Congo)

amur leopard
25–30 left
(eastern Siberia)

black rhino
4800 left
(south central Africa)

kakapo parrot
150 left
(New Zealand)

greater bamboo lemur
250 left
(Madagascar)

Javan rhino
35 left
(Java)

ANIMAL LIFE SPANS

Animals that live the longest

This chart shows you how long different animals live for.

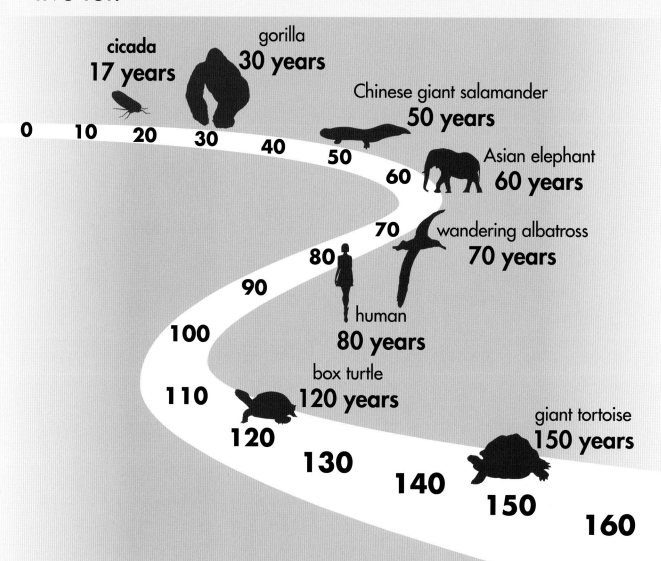

cicada
17 years

gorilla
30 years

Chinese giant salamander
50 years

Asian elephant
60 years

wandering albatross
70 years

human
80 years

box turtle
120 years

giant tortoise
150 years

0   10   20   30   40   50   60   70   80   90   100   110   120   130   140   150   160

Short lives

Some animals live only for a few months. Some only live for a few days! This calendar shows how long five animals all born on 1 January would live for.

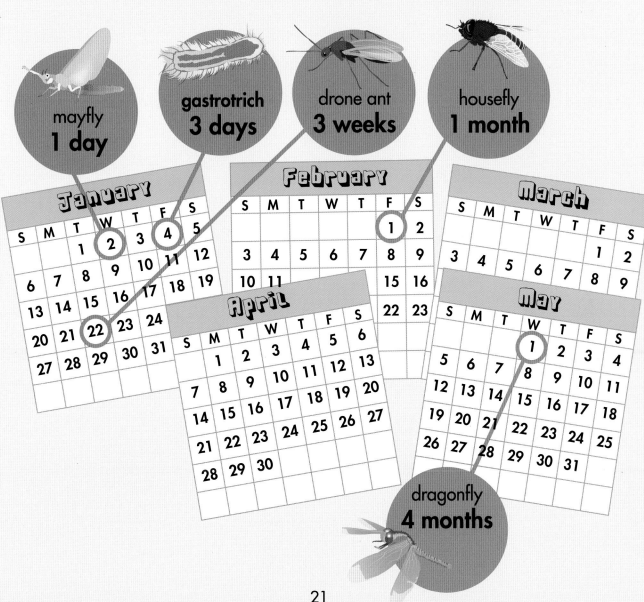

mayfly
1 day

gastrotrich
3 days

drone ant
3 weeks

housefly
1 month

dragonfly
4 months

LIFE CYCLES

The life cycle of an animal can show how the animal is born, lives, and has babies. Here are the life cycles of a frog and a butterfly.

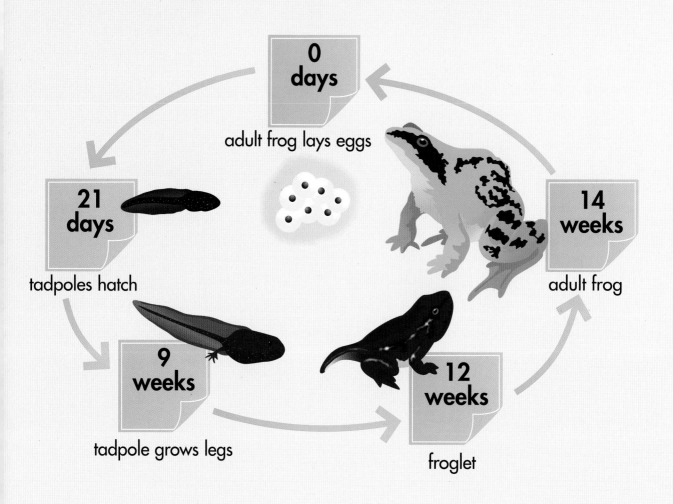

0 days — adult frog lays eggs

21 days — tadpoles hatch

9 weeks — tadpole grows legs

12 weeks — froglet

14 weeks — adult frog

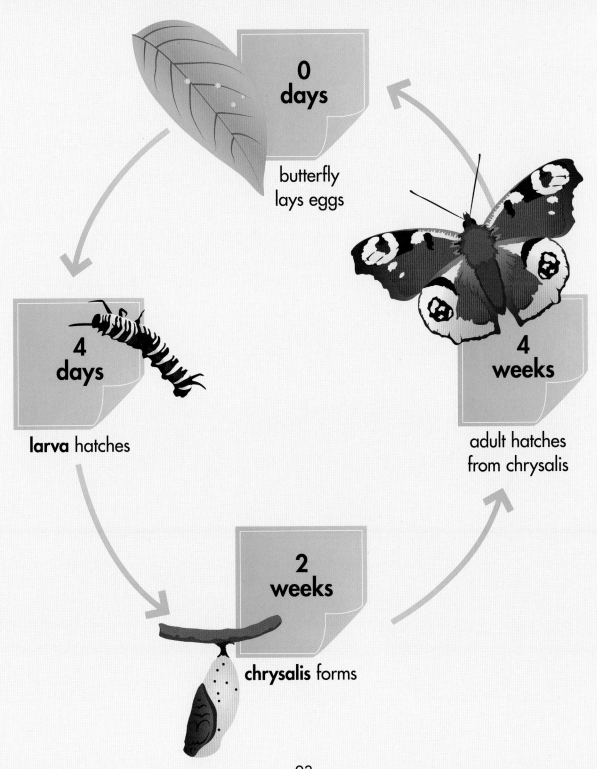

0 days

butterfly lays eggs

4 days

larva hatches

2 weeks

chrysalis forms

4 weeks

adult hatches from chrysalis

23

ANIMAL FOOD

Big dinners

This chart shows how much food different animals have to eat each day to stay alive.

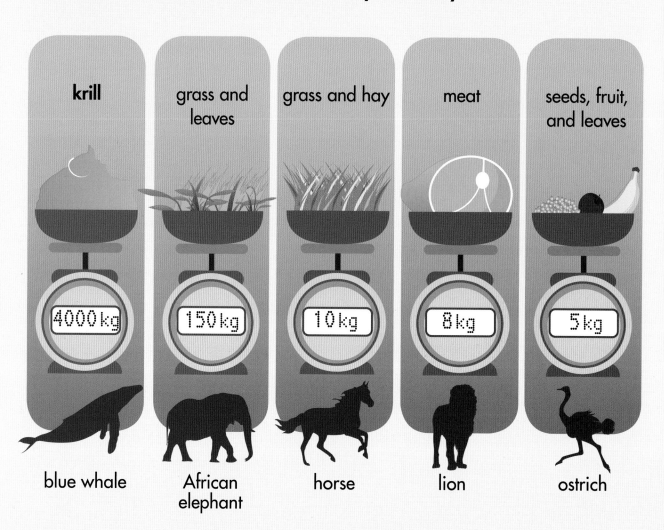

krill	grass and leaves	grass and hay	meat	seeds, fruit, and leaves
4000kg	150kg	10kg	8kg	5kg
blue whale	African elephant	horse	lion	ostrich

What eats what

This chart shows what animals eat plants and other animals. It is called a food web. This food web is for a forest.

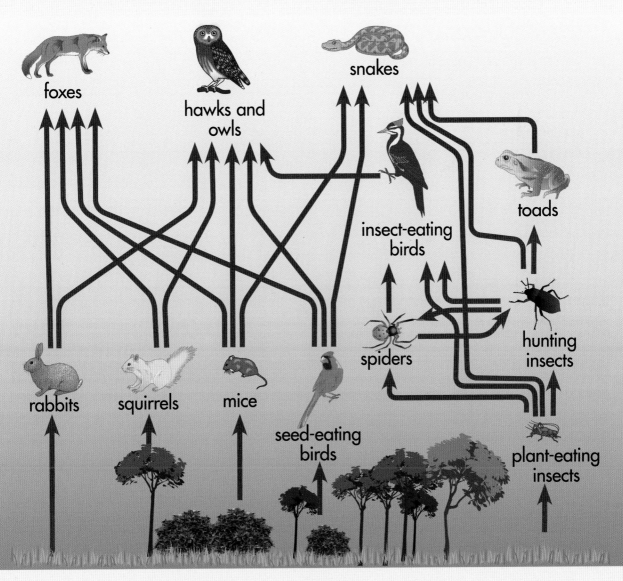

foxes

hawks and owls

snakes

insect-eating birds

toads

hunting insects

spiders

rabbits

squirrels

mice

seed-eating birds

plant-eating insects

LONG JOURNEYS

Many animals make amazingly long journeys to find food and to find places to have their young. These journeys are called **migrations**. This map shows some of the longest migrations.

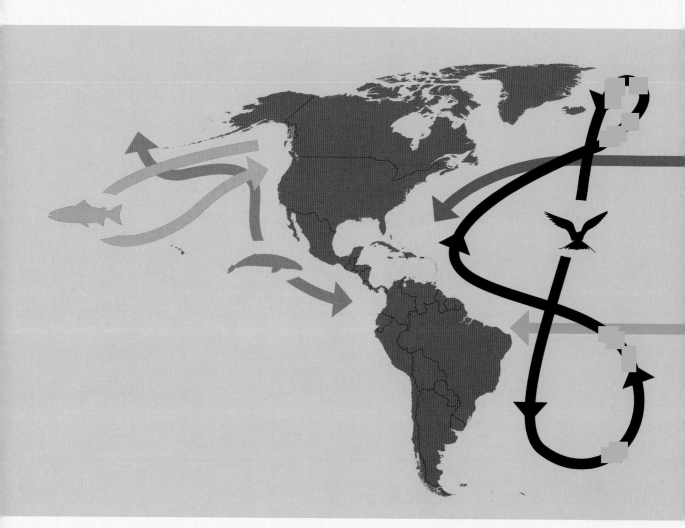

Pacific salmon
11,300 kilometres
into the Pacific and back

European eel
5,000 kilometres
Europe to Sargasso Sea

Arctic tern
70,000 kilometres
Arctic to Antarctic and back

Green turtle
4,500 kilometres
Brazil to Ascension Island
and back

Grey whale
20,000 kilometres
Arctic Ocean to Mexican coast
and back

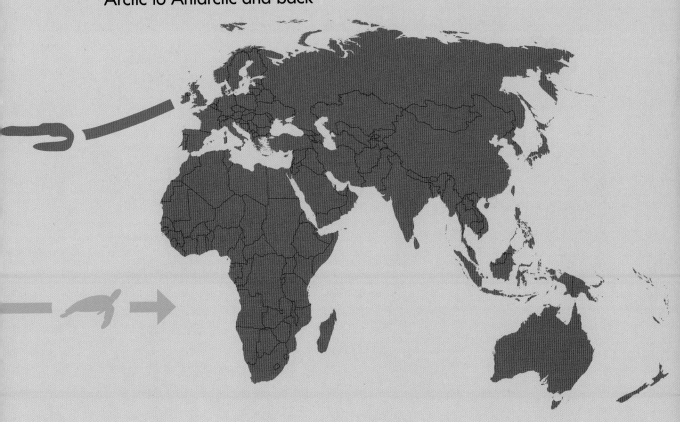

ANIMALS IN THE PAST

Many incredible animals were alive in the past, before humans lived on Earth. This infographic is a timeline that shows when some of these animals lived.

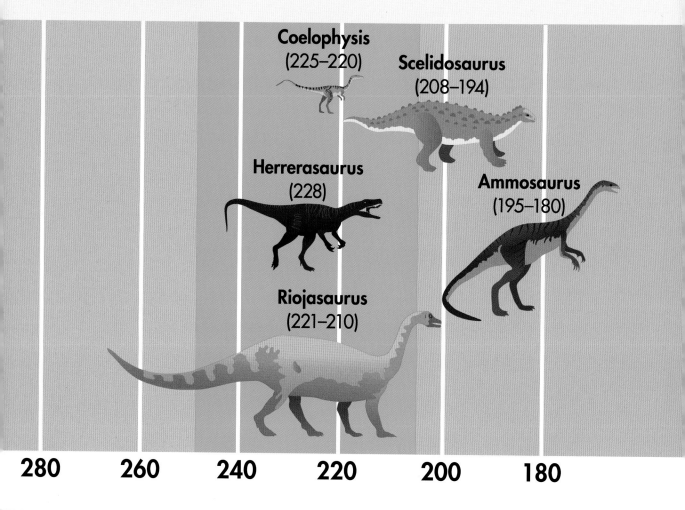

Coelophysis (225–220)

Scelidosaurus (208–194)

Herrerasaurus (228)

Ammosaurus (195–180)

Riojasaurus (221–210)

| 280 | 260 | 240 | 220 | 200 | 180 |

Triassic period 248–206   Jurassic period 206–144

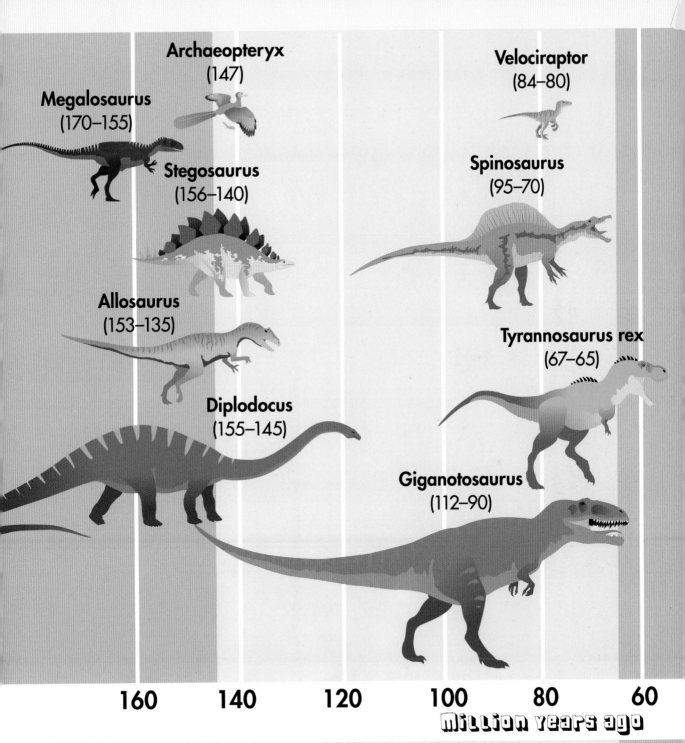

Megalosaurus
(170–155)

Archaeopteryx
(147)

Stegosaurus
(156–140)

Allosaurus
(153–135)

Diplodocus
(155–145)

Velociraptor
(84–80)

Spinosaurus
(95–70)

Tyrannosaurus rex
(67–65)

Giganotosaurus
(112–90)

160   140   120   100   80   60

Million years ago

Cretaceous period 144–65

GLOSSARY

chrysalis hard shell that protects an insect as it changes from a larva to an adult

cicada large flying insect that lives in warm or hot countries

endangered describes an animal that is in danger of dying out

gastrotrich tiny animal that lives in ponds and rivers

krill small shrimp-like animal that lives in the ocean

larva insect before it changes into its adult form. The plural for larva is larvae.

migration long journey from one country or region to another

vaquita small porpoise that lives in the Gulf of California

FIND OUT MORE

Books

101 Animal Records, Melvin and Gilda Berger (Scholastic, 2013)

Making Graphs (series), Vijaya Khisty Bodach (Capstone Press, 2008)

Wild Animals (Horrible Geography Handbooks) Anita Ganeri (Scholastic, 2011)

Websites

animals.nationalgeographic.co.uk/animals/ photos/animal-records-gallery
Find photos and facts about animal record-breakers on this website.

www.bbc.co.uk/bitesize/ks1/maths/ organising_data/play
Visit this website for an interactive activity about making animal graphs.

INDEX